CHICAGO PUBLIC LIBRARY
THOMAS HUGHES CHILDRENS LIBRARY
400 S. STATE ST.   60605

Essential Lives

ABRAHAM LINCOLN

Essential Lives

ABRAHAM LINCOLN

BY KEKLA MAGOON

Content Consultant
Thomas F. Schwartz, Ph.D.
Illinois State Historian
Abraham Lincoln Presidential Library and Museum

ABDO
Publishing Company

Essential Lives

CREDITS

Published by ABDO Publishing Company, 8000 West 78th Street, Edina, Minnesota 55439. Copyright © 2008 by Abdo Consulting Group, Inc. International copyrights reserved in all countries. No part of this book may be reproduced in any form without written permission from the publisher. The Essential Library™ is a trademark and logo of ABDO Publishing Company.

Printed in the United States.

Editor: Rebecca Rowell
Cover Design: Becky Daum
Interior Design: Lindaanne Donohoe

Library of Congress Cataloging-in-Publication Data
Magoon, Kekla.
  Abraham Lincoln / Kekla Magoon.
     p. cm.—(Essential lives)
  Includes bibliographical references and index.
  ISBN 978-1-59928-839-0
  1. Lincoln, Abraham, 1809–1865—Juvenile literature. 2. Presidents—United States—Biography—Juvenile literature. I. Title. II. Series.

E457.905.M315 2008
973.7092—dc22
[B]

2007012268

TABLE OF CONTENTS

Chapter 1	The Road to Greatness	6
Chapter 2	Young Lincoln	14
Chapter 3	Lincoln's Early Political Career	22
Chapter 4	Lincoln as Husband and Father	30
Chapter 5	Lincoln Returns to Politics	38
Chapter 6	To the Presidency	48
Chapter 7	A Nation Divided	58
Chapter 8	Emancipation Proclamation and Gettysburg Address	68
Chapter 9	A Second Term	78
Chapter 10	Assassination and Legacy	86

Timeline	96
Essential Facts	100
Additional Resources	102
Glossary	104
Source Notes	106
Index	108
About the Author	112

Chapter 1

Abraham Lincoln speaks to well-wishers before departing to Washington, D.C., to be sworn in as president of the United States.

The Road to Greatness

On the morning of February 11, 1861, Abraham Lincoln stood on a train platform, staring out at the well-wishers who had gathered to see him off. Lincoln was no stranger to crowds or to making speeches, but he was nervous

Abraham Lincoln

and emotional in this case. He was leaving his hometown of Springfield, Illinois. This crowd was not full of strangers, but friends—people with whom he had lived, worked, laughed, and shared his days. Leaving was harder than he had thought it would be. Lincoln addressed the crowd, saying,

> *To this place, and the kindness of these people, I owe everything. I now leave, not knowing when, or whether ever, I may return, with a task before me greater than that which rested upon Washington ... let us confidently hope that all will yet be well.*[1]

With these words, Lincoln bid the crowd farewell. Then he boarded the train that would take him to Washington, D.C., to be sworn in as the sixteenth president of the United States. The cheers and goodbyes of the people followed him as he went into the train, where his family and travel companions waited for him. The train pulled out of the station, each chug of its wheels taking Lincoln farther from the life he had known. A long journey lay ahead.

The Lincoln Log

Scholars continue to be fascinated by Abraham Lincoln. The Lincoln Log is a day-by-day account of Lincoln's life and activities that students have compiled. It is an amazing resource that includes records of Lincoln's meetings, speeches, travels, and more—down to even minute daily details—such as when he deposited a check at a certain bank or went out to dinner.

Essential Lives

Slave States

Slavery was a major issue for the United States prior to the Civil War. While it had been abolished in the Northern states, slavery was legal and popular in the Southern states. The following states allowed slavery:

Alabama
Arkansas
Florida
Georgia
Kentucky
Louisiana
Maryland
Mississippi
Missouri
North Carolina
South Carolina
Tennessee
Texas
Virginia

Lincoln had been elected president November 6, 1860. He wanted the job, but now he feared that he would not be able to do it as well as it needed to be done. The nation was in turmoil.

For decades, citizens and lawmakers had been debating the issue of slavery in the United States. Slavery had been abolished in the Northern states, but it remained legal and quite popular in the Southern states. Americans were divided about the issue. Some people thought slavery was fine and good because it gave plantation owners a large supply of free laborers. Other people believed slavery was immoral and wanted all slaves freed.

Lincoln opposed the spread of slavery. When he was elected president, several Southern states worried that he would abolish slavery, which would hurt business for the plantation owners. These states believed that the president should not be allowed to end slavery within any state. Rather, the states should be able to decide for themselves whether or not to allow slavery.

Abraham Lincoln

Fearing what Lincoln might do, the Southern states felt they had no choice but to secede from the United States, or Union. These states declared that they were forming their own nation, the Confederate States of America. The Confederate States even elected their own president, Jefferson Davis.

As Lincoln rode the train to Washington, D.C., to begin his presidency, the country was falling apart. Lincoln had not slept well for weeks. He knew the fate of the nation he loved would soon be his responsibility. Lincoln believed the Union must be saved. He could not help but wonder if the task would turn out to be impossible. Or, if it were possible, he worried that he might make mistakes that would cause him to lose the country anyway. Lincoln feared that the nation was on the brink of a civil war.

The train snaked slowly through the North, making dozens of stops along the way. In Illinois, Indiana, Ohio, Pennsylvania, New York, New Jersey, and Maryland, great crowds flocked to see the president-elect pass through. Many citizens had probably seen Lincoln's picture in a newspaper or on his campaign materials, but few had seen him in person.

Lincoln was an unusual-looking man. At 6 feet 4 inches (1.9 m) tall, Lincoln stood out. He liked to wear a stovepipe hat, which made him seem even taller. Lincoln also moved rather awkwardly. His face, when beardless, appeared gaunt, and he had a stern forehead and a long nose. Though he is remembered today with a full beard, Lincoln went without whiskers most of his life. During his presidential campaign, Lincoln received a letter from Grace Bedell, a young girl from Westfield, New York, suggesting that he would look better with a beard. The letter so amused Lincoln that he replied to the little girl personally.

Grace Bedell's Letter

Abraham Lincoln went without facial hair much of his adult life. He decided to grow a beard after receiving a letter from young Grace Bedell. Grace's October 15, 1860, letter follows, including her errors:

> Dear Sir,
> My father has just home from the fair and brought home your picture and Mr. Hamlin's. I am a little girl only eleven years old, but want you should be President of the United States very much so I hope you wont think me very bold to write to such a great man as you are. Have you any little girls about as large as I am if so give them my love and tell her to write to me if you cannot answer this letter. I have got 4 brother's and part of them will vote for you any way and if you will let your whiskers grow I will try and get the rest of them to vote for you. You would look a great deal better for your face is so thin. All the ladies like whiskers and they would tease their husband's to vote for you and then you would be President. My father is a going to vote for you and if I was a man I would vote for you to but I will try and get every one to vote for you that I can I think that rail fence around your picture makes it look very pretty I have got a little baby sister she is nine weeks old and is just as cunning as can be. When you direct your letter dir[e]ct to Grace Bedell Westfield Chatauque County New York
> I must not write any more. Answer this letter right off. Good bye
> Grace Bedell[2]

• 10 •

Abraham Lincoln

When his train passed through her town, Lincoln sought Grace out of the crowd and showed her the whiskers he had grown. "See, I took your advice," he said.[3]

Lincoln met thousands of his supporters on the trip to the nation's capital. At each stop along the way, Lincoln responded to the concerns that were at the front of everyone's mind: slavery, secession, preventing war, and restoring the Union. On the issue of slavery, he would not budge. Lincoln opposed the expansion of slavery. He paid little attention to people who urged him to compromise. He chose not to recognize the secession of the Southern states. In his mind, they remained part of the Union, even if they were a segment of the nation that stood in rebellion against the true government. As to restoring the country, Lincoln deliberately let the American people know that the responsibility of preventing war was not his burden alone. Lincoln vowed that he would not take action to directly cause a civil war, stating,

The Misplaced Speech
Early in Lincoln's train trip to Washington, D.C., to assume office as president of the United States, he became very upset with his oldest son. Robert misplaced the bag containing the draft of Lincoln's inauguration speech, which he had carefully planned. The bag was found, however, and Lincoln's brief show of temper subsided.

Essential Lives

> *To the salvation of this Union there needs but one single thing—the hearts of a people like yours ... my reliance will be placed upon you and the people of the United States. ... It is your business to rise up and preserve the Union and liberty, for yourselves, and not for me.*[4]

Lincoln arrived in Washington, D.C., his new home, on February 23. In just a few days, he would be sworn in as the sixteenth president of the United States.

Lincoln's trip to the nation's capital was over, but his journey as the nation's leader had only just begun. Choices ahead would test the strength of Lincoln's character and the strength of the country. Lincoln took the oath of office March 4, 1861. As he addressed the public for the first time as president, he felt the weight of his office settle on his shoulders. The future was uncertain. Lincoln was not yet a hero, not yet the legend that history would soon make him. He had not yet won the hearts of Americans or built a legacy based on ideals of freedom and democracy. Lincoln was simply a man with an enormous task facing him. All he could do was what he felt was right, which is what he tried to do throughout his life.

Land of Lincoln

Illinois became the United States' twenty-first state December 3, 1818. The state's name is derived from a Native American word that means "tribe of superior men." The state's motto is "State Sovereignty, National Union." The state's slogan is "Land of Lincoln."

Abraham Lincoln

In Memory of
ABRAHAM LINCOLN,
President of the United States of America,
BORN FEBRUARY 12, 1809.
DIED APRIL 15, 1865.

HIS FAREWELL ADDRESS

TO HIS OLD NEIGHBORS.

Springfield, February 12, 1861.

My Friends—

No one not in my position can appreciate the sadness I feel at this parting. To this people I owe all that I am. Here I have lived more than a quarter of a century; here my children were born, and here one of them lies buried. I know not how soon I shall see you again. A duty devolves upon me which is, perhaps, greater than that which has devolved upon any other man since the days of Washington. He never would have succeeded except for the aid of Divine Providence, upon which he at all times relied. I feel that I cannot succeed without the same Divine aid which sustained him, and on the same Almighty Being I place my reliance for support, and I hope you, my friends, will all pray that I may receive that Divine assistance without which I cannot succeed, but with which success is certain. Again I bid you an affectionate farewell.

Lincoln's farewell address to the people of Illinois

Chapter 2

Young Abraham Lincoln reading by the fire

Young Lincoln

Throughout his life, Abraham Lincoln was slow to speak about his upbringing, almost as if he thought it unimportant. Regardless of how Lincoln downplayed his youth, his early experiences surely shaped the man and president he would become.

Abraham Lincoln

Abraham Lincoln was born February 12, 1809, to Thomas and Nancy Lincoln. He was born in a one-room log cabin on his father's farm near Hodgenville, Kentucky. The farm was known as Sinking Spring Farm. As a baby, Abraham lived in the one-room log cabin with his parents and his older sister, Sarah, for a little more than two years.

When Abraham was two years old, his father moved the family to a larger farm on nearby Knob Creek. Thomas Lincoln was a skilled carpenter and a farmer. But he had difficulty keeping the land he purchased because of poor record-keeping and confusion with the Kentucky land titles. He had to go to court several times to defend his ownership of the land. He ultimately lost both the Sinking Spring Farm and Knob Creek properties.

Near Fatal Accident

Abraham Lincoln nearly died at age nine when a horse kicked him in the head. He was knocked unconscious. According to one story, when he woke up, Abraham finished the sentence he had started right before the horse kicked him.

Abraham first witnessed slavery as a child. Several of his mother's relatives owned slaves. Abraham's own family did not, in part because they were poor, but mainly because his father disapproved of owning slaves. Thomas Lincoln even belonged to an anti-slavery Baptist church. In addition to the problems of keeping

Essential Lives

A Love for Animals

Abraham Lincoln loved animals. He had a variety of special childhood pets, including a pig he got from a neighbor and a cat that would walk alongside him each day when he went to the spring to haul water home for his family.

his land, Thomas Lincoln's dislike of the practice of slavery pushed him to move his family away from Kentucky in 1816.

The Lincoln family moved to Indiana, where Thomas Lincoln was able to make a secure land purchase from the federal government. Indiana was a free state, which appealed to him. From age seven, Abraham grew up in southwestern Indiana. The Lincolns lived in the Pigeon Creek community near the Ohio River. Later in life, Abraham Lincoln recalled the hard work of that frontier farm lifestyle. Abraham said upon the family's arrival at their new home, he "had an axe put into his hands at once."[1]

Abraham worked hard alongside his father, chopping trees, plowing, and harvesting. It was also young Abraham's job to fetch water from the creek every day.

In 1818, the Lincoln family was devastated by the death of Abraham's mother. Nancy Hanks Lincoln died from milk sickness, a common ailment caused by drinking milk from a cow that had eaten a poisonous white snakeroot plant. The family struggled without

Abraham Lincoln

a wife and mother for a year or so before Thomas Lincoln decided they needed some help. He left Abraham and Sarah in the care of their older cousin, Dennis Hanks, and returned to Kentucky to find a new wife.

Thomas Lincoln returned to his family several months later with Sarah Bush Johnston Lincoln, his new wife. The new Mrs. Lincoln was a kind woman and loving stepmother for Sarah and Abraham. The family thrived under her care.

From an early age, Abraham set his sights on having a career other than farming. Though he cared for his family and worked hard on the farm every day, Abraham did not want to live the life of his father. Both Thomas Lincoln and his new wife were illiterate and uneducated. Abraham understood that education was vital if he was going to have a different kind of future. He was able to go to school only a little at a time, when farm chores could be put off long enough for him to study. However, his teachers were hardly

Sarah Bush Johnston Lincoln

Born December 13, 1788, in Kentucky, Sarah Bush was one of nine children. When Abraham Lincoln's mother died, his father went back to the Lincolns' home state of Kentucky to find a new wife and a stepmother for his children. Sarah Bush Johnston was a widow with three children. She and Thomas Lincoln wed December 2, 1819. Though he was not close to his father, Abraham and Sarah had a strong connection.

educated themselves. Abraham learned to read, write, and do basic math. Such schooling got him perhaps to the sixth-grade level, which was about average for a farm boy. That was not enough for Abraham. He wanted something different. He was driven by an inner ambition that the people around him did not understand.

Abraham read everything he could get his hands on, though books were scarce where he lived. He sometimes practiced math by writing on the back of a shovel with a lump of coal. Neighbors and friends tended to think Abraham was lazy because he was constantly reading. Abraham's stepmother quietly

---

Lincoln's Autobiography

Abraham Lincoln was a modest and private man, never one to brag about himself. In 1858, Charles Lanman wrote a letter to Lincoln, asking him for an autobiography. Lanman was preparing a *Dictionary of the United States Congress* that would include information on all the current and former members of the U.S. Congress. Lanman did not specify a length for the autobiography he requested. Some Congressmen responded with 20-page narratives about themselves. Lincoln was quite the opposite. He wrote the following:

Born, February 12, 1809, in Hardin County, Kentucky.
Education defective.
Profession, a lawyer.
Have been a captain of volunteers in Black Hawk War.
Postmaster at a very small office.
Four times a member of the Illinois Legislature, and was a member of the lower house of Congress.[2]

encouraged his pursuit of knowledge, even though his father did not understand it. She even saved some of Abraham's scraps of writing, which recorded his youthful thoughts and poetry.

> "If slavery is not wrong, nothing is wrong."[3]
>
> —Abraham Lincoln
> April 4, 1864

As a teenager, Abraham began taking on work beyond his family's farm. He chopped and sold wood to his community. This work was his first attempt to break out of his home existence. In 1928, at age 19, Abraham was hired to help a merchant's son carry a load of produce to New Orleans, Louisiana, on a flatboat down the Mississippi River. During the two-month journey, he again witnessed the conditions of slavery. In one instance, he encountered a group of slaves who attacked his boat and tried to steal the cargo. Abraham's 1928 journey was the first of two raft trips he would take down the Mississippi.

In 1830, the Lincoln family moved from Indiana to Macon County, Illinois. Abraham helped them move and get settled, but he left home shortly thereafter. He made his second raft trip to New Orleans in the spring of 1831. After the trip, he moved to New Salem, Illinois, a small but growing town on the Sangamon River.

Abraham enjoyed his independence but had very few skills apart from his farming experience. He took a job as a store clerk and mill operator. The townspeople came to know him as an honest, intelligent, funny, and clever young man. Eventually, when the store he clerked began to fail, Abraham found himself looking for work again. He considered pursuing various careers, debating between becoming a blacksmith or a lawyer. His interests in law proved much greater, and Abraham turned his attention to politics.

Abraham Lincoln

Sarah Bush Johnston Lincoln, Abraham Lincoln's stepmother

Chapter 3

Lincoln studies under a tree.

Lincoln's Early Political Career

In March 1832, Abraham Lincoln declared his intention to run for political office by becoming a candidate for the Illinois House of Representatives. Lincoln introduced himself to the public as "young and unknown to many of you," but

• 22 •

Abraham Lincoln

someone with a "peculiar ambition ... of being truly esteemed of my fellow men."[1] In a letter printed in the *Sangamo Journal,* a newspaper in Springfield, Illinois, Lincoln described his humble upbringing and asked voters to support his candidacy. Lincoln's platform was based on his experiences transporting goods along the Mississippi River. He also pointed to his experience of keeping the store where he clerked well-stocked. Lincoln believed that government could find ways to transport goods more efficiently, which would benefit small business operations. He studied grammar intently to prepare for the writing and public speaking he knew he would have to do.

Lincoln's Patent

Abraham Lincoln is the only president to hold a patent. His patent was for a system of chambers designed to refloat boats that had run aground. He received Patent 6469 on March 10, 1849.

When he finally lost his job at the store, Lincoln found himself in financial trouble. In April 1832, he decided to join the Illinois militia to fight in the Black Hawk War. The state militia had been called up to drive Chief Black Hawk and his people, the Sauk and Fox tribes, away from the area. At the time, the state militia was a democratic institution that allowed for electing officers. Lincoln's company elected him captain. Lincoln would later say that he was more proud of this particular election than any in his political career, including his election to the presidency. Winning the confidence of his friends and neighbors was "a success that gave me more pleasure than any I have had since," Lincoln said.[2]

Lincoln served in the war for three months, though he never participated in a battle or saw any evidence of Native American hostility. In fact, he once defended an innocent Native American who passed into his company's camp and was nearly killed by the other soldiers. Though uneventful, Lincoln's time in the militia was an important part of his life. The brief

---

Lincoln's Candidacy Letter to the People of Illinois

Announcing his candidacy for representative of Illinois, Lincoln published this letter in the *Sangamo Journal*:

Every man is said to have his peculiar ambition. Whether it be true or not, I can say for one that I have no other so great as that of being truly esteemed of my fellow men, by rendering myself worthy of their esteem. How far I shall succeed in gratifying this ambition is yet to be developed. I am young and unknown to many of you. I was born and have ever remained in the most humble walks of life. I have no wealthy or popular relations to recommend me. My case is thrown exclusively upon the independent voters of this county, and if elected they will have conferred a favor upon me, for which I shall be unremitting in my labors to compensate. But if the good people in their wisdom shall see fit to keep me in the background, I have been too familiar with disappointments to be very much chagrined.

*Your friend and fellow citizen,
A. Lincoln.
New Salem, March 9, 1832*[3]

Abraham Lincoln

experience of leadership cemented his interest in politics and his confidence in his ability to succeed.

Upon leaving the militia, Lincoln's horse was stolen. To get home, he had to walk many miles and travel by canoe. The time he spent traveling was time he had hoped to spend campaigning for the election, and so Lincoln lost the race.

Sangamon County had more than 8,000 voters. Lincoln was unable to get enough votes to win any of the four representative seats that were open. The race had 13 candidates. Pulling a total of 657 votes, Lincoln placed eighth.

Lincoln's interest in politics and law was only strengthened by his loss. He put the old thoughts of becoming a blacksmith behind him for good. Lincoln had won the votes of most of his immediate community (277 out of 300 ballots cast in New Salem). He still was not educated enough to be a lawyer, but he believed in himself enough to want to run for office again. In the meantime, Lincoln needed to find a way to make a living.

Lincoln partnered with a friend, William F. Berry, to purchase a general store. Lincoln had clerking experience, and Berry had a little bit of money. However, the store quickly went into debt. Needing

Essential Lives

other work, Lincoln became postmaster of New Salem in 1833. He also took on work as a county surveyor, teaching himself the skills needed to do the job. Berry died in 1835, leaving Lincoln solely responsible for repaying what they owed on their failed enterprise. It took many years, but Lincoln ultimately repaid the debt.

Lincoln ran for the state legislature a second time in 1834. Again, there were 13 candidates. This time, Lincoln came in second, winning one of the four positions available. As he entered his new role in public office, Lincoln continued to study grammar and literature and honed his oratory skills. John Todd Stuart, a lawyer friend, loaned Lincoln books to study law and encouraged him to work toward his goal. Two years later, Lincoln earned his lawyer's license and took the oath of admission to the Illinois state bar. He moved to Springfield, Illinois, in 1837, where he joined John Todd Stuart's successful law firm.

Lincoln becomes a Lawyer

Becoming a lawyer took Lincoln three steps:

March 24, 1936: Lincoln's name was entered on the Sangamon circuit court record as a person of good moral character.

September 9, 1836: Lincoln was granted a license by two justices of the Illinois Supreme Court that allowed him to practice law in all courts in the state of Illinois.

March 1, 1837: Lincoln's name was entered on the roll of attorneys in the office of the clerk of the Illinois Supreme Court.

• 26 •

Abraham Lincoln

Lincoln went on to serve four terms as a state representative. He worked diligently to improve conditions for Illinois citizens, concentrating on improvements such as building roads, canals, and bridges. His biggest accomplishment was getting the state capital moved from Vandalia to Springfield in 1839.

During most of his time in the state legislature, Lincoln focused on economic development. Occasionally, hints of the convictions that would define his legacy emerged. In 1837, the publisher of an abolitionist newspaper, Elijah Lovejoy, was attacked and murdered in Alton, Illinois, by a mob that then destroyed his printing press. In response, the legislature put forth a resolution condemning abolitionists and affirming the practice of owning slaves as a constitutional right. Lincoln voted against the measure. It ultimately passed, but Lincoln helped write a protest paper arguing that slavery was an injustice.

In January 1838, Lincoln made a speech at the Young Men's Lyceum in Springfield, where he spoke about the ideals of liberty, justice, equality, and a

Honest Abe

Abraham Lincoln is often referred to as "Honest Abe." It is believed that he earned this nickname while working as a store clerk as a young man. Lincoln gave a customer the wrong amount of change. To right his mistake, Lincoln walked a long way to give the customer the correct amount of change.

Essential Lives

Anti-Slavery Argument

On July 1, 1854, Lincoln presented the following anti-slavery argument:

"If A. can prove, however conclusively, that he may, of right, enslave B.—why may not B. snatch the same argument, and prove equally, that he may enslave A?

"You say A. is white, and B. is black. It is color, then; the lighter, having the right to enslave the darker? Take care. By this rule, you are to be slave to the first man you meet, with a fairer skin than your own.

"You do not mean color exactly?—You mean the whites are intellectually the superiors of the blacks, and, therefore have the right to enslave them? Take care again. By this rule, you are to be slave to the first man you meet, with an intellect superior to your own.

"But, say you, it is a question of interest; and, if you can make it your interest, you have the right to enslave another. Very well. And if he can make it his interest, he has the right to enslave you."[4]

united government based on those principles. It was the first time he shifted his message from support for practical measures to his broader beliefs and political ideology. The ideas he presented that night would soon shape his career.

Lincoln was twice offered the opportunity to run for governor of Illinois, but he declined. He may have been set on the U.S. Congress, but he did not initially pursue that either. As a member of the Whig party, Lincoln thought it unlikely that he could be elected to a national office from the mostly Democratic state of Illinois. Still, he continued his work with passion, hoping that such an opportunity would one day present itself.

A different kind of opportunity would soon present itself in Abraham Lincoln's personal life. Her name was Mary Todd.

Abraham Lincoln

Mary Todd

Chapter 4

Abraham Lincoln, 1846

Lincoln as Husband and Father

Abraham Lincoln met Mary Todd in December 1839 at a cotillion in Springfield. He was awkward and shy around most women, so dating was difficult. He did have a friendship once with Ann Rutledge, the tavern owner's daughter back in New Salem. He was even engaged to a woman named Mary Owens, though the couple never married.

Mary Todd was from Lexington, Kentucky. She was in Springfield visiting her sister. As a young lawyer, Lincoln would surely have been considered a catch. Despite his modest upbringing, he had achieved prominent status in the community. Todd came from a wealthy and distinguished family. Lincoln once commented on the Todd family's confidence in their own social standing by joking that "one D was enough for God, but not the Todds."[1]

Though he associated with the well-to-do Todd family, the naturally modest Lincoln never thought himself above anyone. He considered himself a common man, even as he became famous. Mary Todd's upper-class background came in handy as Lincoln became more well known. She helped him learn manners appropriate for a lawyer and politician. During his rural upbringing, Lincoln had not learned the rules for how to behave in polite society.

Lincoln as Lawyer

Lincoln was a successful lawyer. He first joined John T. Stuart's law firm in 1837, but they ended the partnership four years later. Lincoln then joined another firm with Stephen T. Logan. In 1844, Lincoln left that partnership to form his own office, where he brought William Herndon on as a junior partner.

When Lincoln proposed marriage to Todd, she accepted. Some of her family members seemed to consider Lincoln too unpolished to be a good husband. Lincoln broke off their engagement. Both he and Todd were so brokenhearted that they eventually resumed their relationship.

Abraham Lincoln and Mary Todd wed November 4, 1842. The first home they shared was a single room at the Globe Tavern in Springfield. They paid $4 per week for the room. Their first son, Robert Todd Lincoln, was born there August 1, 1843.

In 1844, the couple purchased a house. Lincoln's

A Presidential Pardon

Lincoln always made time for his sons. He was an indulgent, affectionate, and wise parent. He made toys for the boys, and let them run around his law office, much to the annoyance of his law partner, William H. Herndon.

Even later, as president, Lincoln paid the boys a great deal of attention. Their energetic play kept White House staff always on alert. A favorite game the boys developed during the Civil War involved a soldier doll named Jack. The boys regularly led Jack on marches and into battle, occasionally even putting him on trial for desertion. Jack was usually found guilty, executed, and buried beneath the rose bushes in the yard. Eventually, the White House gardener reached his limit with the game of burying and unburying Jack. He suggested that the boys appeal to their father on Jack's behalf for a presidential pardon. They scampered into the Oval Office, begging Lincoln to hear Jack's case. Lincoln put aside the serious concerns of his office for a moment to listen to the boys' request. When they finished, Lincoln nodded thoughtfully. He jotted a quick note: "The doll Jack is pardoned. By order of the President."[2]

successful law practice provided a comfortable life for the family. Still, Mary Todd Lincoln's wealthy southern upbringing had not fully prepared her for life as a wife and mother in a family without servants to assist her. The Todd family had slaves who helped with the household chores. Of course, the Lincolns would never own slaves, and they generally did not have hired help.

The Lincolns' second child, Edward Baker Lincoln, was born March 10, 1846. As a father, Lincoln was very different from his own father. Lincoln was gentle and affectionate, making time for his children despite having a busy schedule. He encouraged education for them, particularly Robert, whom he sent to boarding school and then Harvard University.

Lincoln's interest in politics began to extend to the national level, but it was still difficult for a Whig to get elected to national office from Illinois. Not enough people would vote for him. Lincoln and several other

> **Defending Duff Armstrong**
>
> As a lawyer, Lincoln defended a man named Duff Armstrong, who was tried for murder in Illinois in 1858. The prosecution brought forth a witness who claimed he had seen the killing take place by the light of a full moon overhead. Lincoln asked the witness to repeat his story. He then showed an almanac to prove that the moon had been low that day. If the witness was wrong about the moon, Lincoln suggested to the jury, he could certainly be wrong about other things. The jury deliberated for one hour. They found Duff Armstrong not guilty.

Whig candidates got together to try to solve the problem. They decided to join forces to get one man elected, instead of running several Whigs in one race. When it was Lincoln's turn, the other candidates asked their supporters to vote for Lincoln to give him a better chance in the race. They also helped him campaign.

In 1846, Lincoln ran for Congress against Democrat Peter Cartwright. Cartwright was a Methodist circuit rider, a traveling preacher who spent time in several different towns throughout the year. Because of Cartwright's connection with religion, Lincoln's own religious beliefs became an issue in the campaign. Lincoln was accused of condemning Christianity because he was not a practicing Christian. Many people grew skeptical of his different view of God and faith. Lincoln replied to the public's concerns in a letter published as a handbill. He wrote,

> *That I am not a member of any Christian Church, is true, but I have never denied the truth of the Scriptures, and I have never spoken with intentional disrespect of religion in general or of any denomination of Christians. ... I do not think I could myself, be brought to support a man for office, whom I knew to be an open enemy of, and scoffer at, religion.*[3]

Abraham Lincoln

Lincoln was elected to the U.S. House of Representatives in August 1846. The Thirtieth Congress convened in December 1847. During his time in office, Lincoln was disturbed by the presence of slaves in the District of Columbia. He tried to get laws passed to ban the slave trade in Washington, D.C. He also introduced a law that would free enslaved children born after 1850, with a goal of gradually eliminating slavery. None of his efforts were successful. At the end of his term, Lincoln left Congress without having accomplished much. He was disappointed. The experience of governing had not been what he had expected it to be. Lincoln probably would have liked another chance at the job, but he had agreed to rotate the seat with the other Whigs from Illinois.

Lincoln thought President Zachary Taylor, a fellow Whig, might offer him a lucrative position in his administration. However, Lincoln was offered a lower post that did not interest him. In 1849, he returned to Springfield. Lincoln's return coincided with a tragic event in his family life. Abraham and Mary Lincoln's second son, Eddie, died

Fee for Legal Services

In 1857, Lincoln received the largest single fee for his legal services—$4,800—for representing Illinois County Railroad.

Mary Todd

Mary Ann Todd, Abraham Lincoln's wife, was born in Lexington, Kentucky, December 13, 1818. She was the fourth of seven children in her family. Her father, Robert Smith Todd, was a prominent citizen who owned a successful store and served as a state senator. Mary's mother, Eliza Parker Todd, died when Mary was only six years old. Mary was well-educated, having attended private schools for girls.

from a lung illness February 1, 1850. He was only three years old. The Lincolns would have two more sons within three years of Eddie's death. William Wallace Lincoln was born December 21, 1850. The youngest child, Thomas "Tad" Lincoln, was born April 4, 1853. Lincoln tirelessly dedicated himself to his growing family and his legal practice. Lincoln's law practice with William H. Herndon was becoming quite successful. For a time, Abraham Lincoln had grown tired of politics.

Abraham Lincoln

Mary Todd Lincoln with sons Willie and Tad

Abraham Lincoln and Stephen Douglas debated seven times in the fall of 1858 while campaigning for a seat on the U.S. Senate.

Lincoln Returns to Politics

Passage of the Kansas-Nebraska Act on May 30, 1854, brought Lincoln back into politics with vigor. The new law supported the expansion of slavery into the unsettled West. It also overturned the Missouri Compromise of 1820, which

Abraham Lincoln

had prohibited slavery in the northern sections of U.S. land acquired in the Louisiana Purchase. The Kansas-Nebraska Act would allow new western states to choose whether they wanted to enter the Union as slave states or free states. The act had been introduced by Stephen A. Douglas, and there was much debate before it became a law.

Lincoln was shocked by the decision. He believed that if the nation could stop the westward spread of slavery, slavery would die out. In his early campaigns, even though he was against slavery, Lincoln had spoken only about stopping the spread of slavery, not about emancipating slaves.

The huge Louisiana Territory purchased by the United States in 1803 included land that would become Kansas, Nebraska, Montana, Colorado, Wyoming, North Dakota, and South Dakota. If this land was opened to slave owners, Lincoln feared that these regions would choose to be slave states if given the option.

The Caning of Sumner
In May 1856, Senator Charles Sumner of Massachusetts spoke out against bloody partisan warfare that resulted when the Kansas-Nebraska Act was passed. After the Senate adjourned for the day, Sumner was beaten with a cane by Preston Brooks, representative from South Carolina, right in the Senate chamber. Brooks resigned after the incident. Sumner recovered and returned to work. He served 18 more years.

Senator Douglas wanted residents of a state to have the right to vote their state either slave or free. He called the concept "popular sovereignty."

Lincoln so fundamentally disagreed with this support of slavery that he re-entered the political scene with fierce energy. He spoke out against Douglas in a series of speeches in which Lincoln voiced his stance against the Kansas-Nebraska Act. Lincoln was elected to state legislature for a fifth term in 1854. But he declined the seat because it would make him ineligible to run against Douglas for the U.S. Senate.

By this time, Lincoln was well known within his community and throughout Illinois. However, a popular vote was not required to win him the Senate seat. At the time, senators were voted into office by their state legislatures. The Illinois State Legislature was dominated by Democrats. Lincoln's Whig party could not get him elected. Though he had many legislators' votes in his favor, they were not enough. Lincoln ultimately withdrew from the race, encouraging his supporters to vote for the anti-Nebraska Democrat who won the seat.

"Although volume upon volume is written to prove slavery a very good thing, we never hear of the man who wishes to take the good of it, by being a slave himself."[1]

—Abraham Lincoln

Abraham Lincoln

Lincoln and Douglas debate

    Lincoln's Whig party became seriously divided over slavery in the wake of the Kansas-Nebraska Act. One section of Whigs broke off and joined a group that called itself the Know-Nothing Party. Lincoln criticized the Know-Nothings for being anti-slavery and anti-immigrant at the same time. Lincoln joined another group of anti-slavery Whigs, who partnered with anti-slavery Democrats and joined a new group called the Republican Party. Lincoln was sorry to see the Whigs collapse in this way. He was skeptical about the possibility of success with the Republican Party, but he continued to help establish the group. The first Republican national convention was held in 1856.

The 1857 *Dred Scott* decision by the U.S. Supreme Court increased tensions around slavery. Dred Scott and his wife were slaves in Missouri who filed a lawsuit to obtain their freedom. The Supreme Court ruled that no slave could be a U.S. citizen. Therefore, slaves and their children had no rights in the country. Lincoln

Lincoln-Douglas Debates of 1858

Illinois Senator Stephen A. Douglas proposed the Kansas-Nebraska Act, which would allow each of the new western states formed from the Louisiana Purchase to choose to be a slave state or a free state. Abraham Lincoln strongly opposed the expansion of slavery the act could ultimately allow and was shocked when it became a law May 30, 1854. Lincoln expressed his disapproval of the law in what were known as "anti-Nebraska" speeches.

Lincoln opposed Douglas in the race for the U.S. Senate seat. In the fall of 1858, Lincoln and Douglas debated seven times while campaigning. They met in different cities throughout Illinois:

August 21: Ottawa
August 21: Freeport
September 15: Jonesboro
September 18: Charleston
October 7: Galesburg
October 13: Quincy
October 15: Alton

Abraham Lincoln

called the decision a mockery of the principle that "all men are created equal."[2]

Lincoln ran against Douglas for a Senate seat in 1858, this time as a Republican. Lincoln launched his campaign at the Republican convention with a speech in which he proclaimed that "a house divided against itself cannot stand."[3] He was referring to the different views of slavery that existed in the country. A nation made up of half slave states and half free states was a house divided, especially with slave owners so deeply committed to slavery, and radical abolitionists rising up against it. Lincoln foresaw, as many people did, that the country was heading for a difficult crossroads.

Since Douglas already held the office, he had an advantage over Lincoln in the Senate race. Lincoln knew he had to give voters a chance to get to know him and to compare his views with Douglas's. He challenged Douglas to debate him on the issue of slavery. Douglas agreed. The men met several times to debate before voters throughout Illinois. The seven encounters

> "A house divided against itself cannot stand. I believe this government cannot endure, permanently half slave and half free. I do not expect the Union to be dissolved—I do not expect the house to fall—but I do expect it will cease to be divided."[4]
>
> —Abraham Lincoln

The Lincoln-Douglas debate in Galesburg, Illinois, drew a large crowd.

between the two candidates became the famous Lincoln-Douglas Debates of 1858.

Lincoln and Douglas debated in seven Illinois towns during August, September, and October 1858. The debates were long—about three hours each—but exciting. People traveled from miles around to see the candidates speak. They stood out in blazing summer heat and cold fall weather to hear what Lincoln and

Abraham Lincoln

Douglas had to say. On the day of each debate, there were parades, other speakers, and festivities. Tens of thousands of people participated in the day's events.

Lincoln was an eloquent debater. He challenged the logic of slavery and questioned the legal basis for it. Douglas billed himself as not necessarily pro-slavery but in favor of letting states decide the issue for themselves. Political cartoonists drew mocking pictures of Lincoln and Douglas debating. The images usually depicted Lincoln as ridiculously long and thin with his characteristic stovepipe hat and Douglas as short and toad-like with flapping coattails. The entire state was caught up in the dramatic exchanges. Despite Lincoln's success in the debates, it was not enough to win the election. Douglas retained his position as senator.

Lincoln was sorely disappointed by the loss, but he kept his public persona positive and confident. He did not give up on the local politics that had brought him such success. However, he also recognized that his strong anti-slavery position in the debates had brought him some national attention. He had transcripts of the debates published so that they could be read more widely.

Lincoln continued to practice law and speak out against slavery. He knew the nation was in turmoil over

> "This declared indifference ... for the spread of slavery, I cannot but hate. I hate it for the monstrous injustice of slavery itself. I hate it because it deprives our republican example of its just influence in the world—enables the enemies of free institutions, with plausibility, to taunt us as hypocrites—causes real friends of freedom to doubt our sincerity, and especially because it forces so many really good men amongst ourselves into an open war with the very fundamental principles of civil liberty—criticizing the Declaration of Independence, and insisting that there is no right principle of action but self-interest."[6]
>
> —Abraham Lincoln

this issue, but he was reasonably content to have had "a hearing on the great and durable question of the age" by sharing his opinions in the debates.[5] At the time, he probably had no idea of the huge political challenges that lay just ahead for him.

Abraham Lincoln

Abraham Lincoln, 1858

Chapter 6

The 1860 Republican convention was held in Chicago.

To the Presidency

In April 1859, Lincoln wrote to other Republican leaders, "I must, in candor, say I do not think myself fit for the Presidency."[1]

The Republican Party had shown interest in him as a possible candidate for vice president, and perhaps even

Abraham Lincoln

for president, but Lincoln did not believe he had enough national prominence to make a successful campaign. Lincoln got his chance to gain national recognition when he was invited to speak at Cooper Union, a prestigious school in New York City, in February 1860. Lincoln understood the opportunity that lay before him. He worked carefully on his speech. He even bought a new suit for the occasion, wanting to impress the sophisticated audience. It was an important occasion. The Cooper Union speech would ultimately be one of the defining moments of Lincoln's political career. He closed his remarks with an idea that resonated with the crowd, saying,

The Wide Awakes

Many young men supported Lincoln's campaign. One group of young men, the Wide Awakes, would march through the streets at night in torchlit processions. The group helped raise funds and spread the word about Lincoln and other Republican candidates.

> *Let us have faith that right makes might and in that faith let us, to the end, dare to do our duty as we understand it.* [2]

The speech was so exciting and moving to the crowd that it was printed in all the local papers and pamphlets. Lincoln was thrust into the national spotlight as a possibility for the Republican nomination for president, or at least for vice president. After Cooper

Union, he went on to give nine more speeches in the Northeast.

The 1860 Republican national convention took place in March in Chicago, Illinois. Lincoln and the other candidates did not attend, but their supporters turned out in full force. Lincoln wanted badly to go to the convention, but it would have been improper.

Lincoln was not the frontrunner for the presidential nomination, but he was certainly a favorite. At the convention, he gained the nomination almost by accident. At first, no candidate—including Lincoln— had enough votes to win. However, the other candidates' supporters refused to change their votes to support William Seward, the candidate who was expected to win the nomination. Because of what some supporters considered a radical past, they wanted Seward to lose almost as much as they wanted their own candidates to win. Some of the other candidates' supporters began voting for Lincoln, believing that a more unknown candidate would be the lesser of two evils between Lincoln and Seward.

When the vote for Lincoln was finalized, celebrations broke out in the streets of Chicago and in towns across the North. The enthusiasm for Lincoln was a promising sign for the upcoming election. Back

Abraham Lincoln

home in Springfield, Lincoln received a telegram at the *Illinois State Journal* office announcing him as the Republican presidential candidate. He rushed home to share the news with Mary, and then they waited.

Unlike the politicians of today, presidential candidates in Lincoln's day remained largely out of public view during the campaigns. Lincoln remained home with his family while other Republican Party leaders made speeches and campaigned on his behalf. Of course, he was involved in the campaign from behind the scenes. He wrote letters, planned strategies with party members, and responded to the many people who reached out to him during those months, including journalists, artists, well-wishers, and concerned citizens.

Lincoln had three opponents in the race. One was Democratic candidate Stephen A. Douglas, the man to whom he had lost the U.S. Senate race. One was John C. Breckinridge, who had been nominated by a group of southern Democrats. The third, John Bell, was

Rail Splitter

In the 1860 presidential campaign, Lincoln became known as "Rail Splitter." Originally given by an opponent, the nickname was meant as a criticism, but it turned out to help Lincoln's campaign. He had spent years splitting wood for fence rails as a youth in Indiana and as a young man in Illinois. Instead of putting off people, it made Lincoln seem down-to-earth and understanding of common struggles.

nominated by leaders of the border states—Kentucky, Tennessee, and Virginia—who feared a civil war over slavery.

The 1860 presidential election would affect the nation's entire future. Voters surely knew this when they went to the polls. Douglas won in Missouri and New Jersey. Breckinridge won in 11 Southern states. Bell won in the border states. Lincoln's name had not even been listed on the ballot in many of the Southern states, but he won nearly all the Northern states, which gave him enough electoral college points to win the election.

The Confederacy

Angered over Lincoln's stance on slavery, South Carolina seceded, or separated, from the Union in late December of 1860. Within six months, ten states joined South Carolina and created their own Confederate States of America, complete with a president, Jefferson Davis. Following are the states of the Confederacy in order of secession:

South Carolina: December 20, 1860
Mississippi: January 9, 1861
Florida: January 10, 1861
Alabama: January 11, 1861
Georgia: January 19, 1861
Louisiana: January 26, 1861
Texas: February 1, 1861
Virginia: April 17, 1861
Arkansas: May 6, 1861
Tennessee: May 7, 1861
North Carolina: May 20, 1861

The Confederacy had its own flag. In fact, it had three flags over the years:

1. "Stars and Bars" was the flag from March 1861 to May 1863.

2. "Stainless Banner" was the flag from May 1863 to March 1865.

3. "Final Edition" was the flag from March to April 1865.

Abraham Lincoln

Immediately upon being elected, Lincoln felt the heavy task of leading the struggling nation fall on his shoulders. He took the responsibility seriously, and he was nervous about the challenge. Lincoln took an office in the state capitol, where he worked during the last four months of James Buchanan's presidency. Lincoln was preparing for his turn to be president of the United States.

Meanwhile, the differences of opinion between the North and South grew deeper. People in both regions feared the possibility of a civil war. They urged Lincoln to consider a compromise. Lincoln could do little but make promises from his position as president-elect, and he chose to stay quiet. He held firm to the central principle of the Republican Party platform by opposing the expansion of slavery. He understood that his decision might lead to a split between the states, but

Border States

The following states had strong ties to both the North and the South:

Delaware
Kentucky
Maryland
Missouri
Virginia
West Virginia (split from Virginia in 1863)

Union States

Thirteen states were considered part of the Union, or North:

Connecticut
Illinois
Indiana
Iowa
Maine
Massachusetts
New Hampshire
New Jersey
New York
Ohio
Pennsylvania
Rhode Island
Vermont

he believed that a compromise would only delay the inevitable.

On December 20, 1860, about a month after Lincoln's election win, South Carolina seceded from the Union. Several other Southern states soon announced their intention to secede. Lincoln still refused to compromise. He wrote to other Republicans, urging them to stand fast on the issue of slavery. He seemed to believe that, in the long run, Southerners would be more committed to the Union than to the institution of slavery. He was wrong.

On February 11, 1861, Lincoln bid an emotional farewell to his friends, colleagues, and supporters in Springfield. He and his family were heading to Washington, D.C., to begin the transition into the White House. The stirring speech he delivered at the train depot hinted to the fact that he would never return. On some level, the departure must have felt permanent to Lincoln. He certainly intended to come back to live and work in Illinois once his term as president was completed, however.

The Lincoln family's journey to the nation's capital included many stops. Their train took a long route, passing through Indiana, Ohio, Pennsylvania, New York, New Jersey, and Maryland before arriving in

Abraham Lincoln

Washington, D.C. In each town, crowds gathered to see Lincoln. He greeted the people warmly and with confidence that he would help make things right within the country. As the train passed through Baltimore, Maryland, threats of assassination by angry Southerners made the travelers nervous. Lincoln took a different train than he had planned, and he arrived in Washington, D.C., without ceremony. Some people called his actions cowardly. Lincoln must have decided these people were right because he never again allowed threats of assassination to affect his plans.

On March 4, 1861, Abraham Lincoln took the oath of office of the president of the United States. That day, he stood on the steps of the half-built Capitol building. Under the protection of cavalry, artillery, and riflemen, he delivered his inaugural address. In that speech, Lincoln pledged his devotion to the Union, promising that he would not start a war. He referred to the oath he had just taken to "preserve, protect, and defend" the Constitution and the nation,

Presidential Oath of Office

Article II, Section 1 of the U.S. Constitution details the swearing in of the president:

"Before he enter on the execution of his office, he shall take the following oath or affirmation: 'I do solemnly swear (or affirm) that I will faithfully execute the office of President of the United States, and will to the best of my ability, preserve, protect and defend the Constitution of the United States.'"[3]

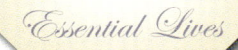

and he appealed to the citizens to remain united, saying,

> *In your hands, my dissatisfied countrymen, and not in mine, is the momentous issue of civil war. The Government will not assail you. You can have no conflict without being yourselves the aggressors. You have no oath registered in heaven to destroy the Government, while I shall have the most solemn one to "preserve, protect, and defend it."*

> *I am loath to close. We are not enemies but friends. We must not be enemies. Though passion may have strained, it must not break our bonds of affection. The mystic chords of memory, stretching from every battlefield and patriot grave to every living heart and hearthstone all over this broad land, will yet swell the chorus of the Union, when again touched, as surely they will be, by the better angels of our nature.*[4]

The country was on edge. Seven Southern states had seceded from the Union. They formed a new government with its own military, calling themselves the Confederate States of America. The Union that Lincoln sought to protect no longer existed.

Abraham Lincoln

Abraham Lincoln at Cooper Union

Abraham Lincoln with Union troops at Antietam in Maryland

A Nation Divided

Civil war was imminent. Although his fear of war was on its way to being realized, Lincoln took seriously his inauguration pledge not to initiate hostilities. And he still held the responsibility of protecting the Union when and where he could.

Abraham Lincoln

The seceding states had taken hold of most of the forts in the South for Confederate use. Fort Sumter in South Carolina still remained in Union hands, under the command of Major Robert Anderson. Anderson refused to surrender the fort to Confederate forces. The South Carolina government saw this resistance as an act of war. State leaders demanded the release of the fort, but Anderson held fast.

Lincoln supported Anderson's stand, but he could not send additional forces to reinforce the fort's defense. The Confederates might read that as an act of war. Lincoln found himself caught between the need to defend Union property and his promise to not contribute to the start of a civil war. When he learned that Fort Sumter's food and supplies were low, Lincoln decided to send supplies but not troops.

The First to Fall

The Union's first commissioned officer killed in the Civil War was a personal friend of Lincoln, Colonel Elmer Ellsworth. Ellsworth was from Illinois and had traveled on the president-elect's train to Washington, D.C., for the inauguration. On May 24, 1861, Ellsworth led a volunteer regiment of New York City firemen across the Potomac River from Washington, D.C., into Alexandria, Virginia. The regiment went to a particular hotel and climbed its roof to take down a Confederate flag that was visible from the White House. As the troops climbed down the building, the hotel owner shot at Ellsworth, killing him. Ellsworth's body was laid in state at the White House, and Lincoln wrote a personal condolence letter to his family.

Essential Lives

On April 9, 1861, a fleet of ships filled with supplies left New York and headed for South Carolina. Three days later, the Union ships sailed into Charleston Harbor to deliver the cargo to Fort Sumter. Upon their arrival, Confederate forces fired on Fort Sumter. The American Civil War had begun.

On April 14, Fort Sumter fell to the Confederates. The next day, Lincoln called for 75,000 volunteers to help fight for the Union. He also called Congress into a special session, which was set to begin July 4. On April 19, he closed all the ports on the Southern coast. Lincoln's emergency actions in the face of the attack on Fort Sumter led to Virginia's immediate secession from the Union. Within a month, Tennessee, Arkansas, and North Carolina followed. Lincoln quickly negotiated with leaders in the border states of Maryland and Kentucky, hoping to keep them in the Union. His tactics worked.

The First First Lady

Mary Todd Lincoln was the first presidential wife to be commonly referred to as First Lady.

Tens of thousands of young men flocked to join the armies in both the North and South, eager to defend their homes and country. Responding with full-fledged support of Lincoln's defense efforts, Congress approved his requests for funds and soldiers when it

Abraham Lincoln

Citizens of Charleston, South Carolina, watch Fort Sumter burn at the start of the Civil War.

convened in July. Congress even increased the number of volunteers from the 400,000 Lincoln requested to 500,000.

The first field battle of the Civil War occurred July 21, 1861. Union and Confederate troops met in the

Battle of Bull Run in Manassas, Virginia. Neither side had had enough time to prepare their soldiers for fighting. Passionate but unprepared young troops marched onto the battlefield. Many did not walk off. More than 800 men died. Two thousand more were injured. Everyone—citizens, soldiers, legislators, and Lincoln himself—was shocked by the sheer number of casualties.

The Confederate troops won at Bull Run, with Union troops retreating after a day of fighting. The Union's army returned to Washington, D.C., to regroup. The catastrophic loss inspired Lincoln to look for new

The Lincoln Penny

The Lincoln penny was issued on August 2, 1909. It was the first American coin with a president's likeness. Previous coins had only shown national symbols, such as eagles and stars. Theodore Roosevelt, then president, asked artist Victor David Brenner to create the coin on the anniversary of Lincoln's 100th birthday.

The Lincoln penny entered the scene surrounded by controversy. Some people thought putting his face on a coin made Lincoln seem too much like a king. Some Southerners resented the choice of Lincoln as a representative of the nation. The first minting of the coin carried the artist's initials, VDB, which also had never been done on a coin before. People did not like it. Only 22 million coins were struck with Brenner's initials.

The original design of the penny was Lincoln's profile on the coin's face, and two stalks of wheat on the back. The wheat design was meant to represent America's plenty. In 1959, the wheat design was replaced with an image of the Lincoln Memorial, in honor of the 150th anniversary of Lincoln's birth.

Abraham Lincoln

military leadership. He turned to Major General George B. McClellan, who took command of the Army of the Potomac, the forces protecting Washington, D.C. McClellan was reluctant to move the Union forces forward, but Lincoln was left with few other options.

Lincoln promoted McClellan to general-in-chief of all the armies November 1, 1861. Shortly thereafter, McClellan became seriously ill. Lincoln took matters into his own hands and tried to manage the war himself. He found that communication was poor between his generals, and strategic planning within the war effort had substantial flaws. The strength and efficiency of Confederate generals Robert E. Lee and Thomas "Stonewall" Jackson had quickly given the South the upper hand. Heading into 1862, the situation was bleak for Lincoln.

To make matters worse, Lincoln's 11-year-old son, Willie, died February 20, 1862, following a three-week illness. Willie's death devastated the family. Mary Lincoln fell into a deep mourning that lasted for more than a year.

Lincoln's White House

Lincoln's lively family brought the White House activity it had not seen in many years. Lincoln was the first president in a long time to have an active first lady as well as young children. Young Willie and Tad especially kept the mansion's staff at attention.

As commander in chief, Lincoln could not afford to let his grief overcome him. He had to deal with the concerns of an entire nation. Lincoln studied military science from textbooks he borrowed from the Library of Congress, believing that if he educated himself, he would be better able to lead the war effort. During the first year of the war, Lincoln was cautious about passing slavery laws. He worried that too much talk about emancipation could hurt the war effort in the North. Also, his position throughout his political career had been to oppose the spread of slavery, not to abolish it where it already existed.

Death Threats

Abraham Lincoln received hundreds of letters from people who hated him and wanted to see him dead. About these threats, Lincoln said, "I long ago made up my mind that if anyone wants to kill me, he will do it. I know I'm in danger but I'm not going to worry about it."[1]

As the war progressed, Lincoln changed his position on freeing slaves. The war had already changed the lives of many slaves. For instance, not all slaves fleeing into the Union were set free. Many Union generals returned slaves to their masters. It was only later in the war that a uniform policy was set.

On July 22, 1862, Lincoln read a draft of an emancipation proclamation to his closest advisors, his Cabinet members. The proclamation would end

Abraham Lincoln

slavery in the United States. The men were stunned at Lincoln's change of heart. They were very nervous about what emancipation would mean to the nation. The Cabinet members advised Lincoln not to announce the proclamation just yet. The Union was losing the war. If Lincoln presented an emancipation proclamation at that moment, the Cabinet members feared that it would appear to be the desperate final act of a dying administration.

While the Emancipation Proclamation seems to represent Lincoln's personal wish that "all men everywhere be free," his decision to deliver it at all was more strategic than moral. He did not want a Union with any trace of slavery. Over time, the war changed people's attitudes and most people saw a connection between slavery and the war. Lincoln's primary goal as president and in crafting the Emancipation Proclamation was to save the Union, writing to journalist and politician Horace Greeley in August 1862, "My paramount object in this struggle is to save the Union, and is not either to save or destroy slavery."[2]

Lincoln thought focusing on abolition would rally the troops, who were feeling disheartened by their lack of success in the war. Ending slavery would help him achieve that goal.

Essential Lives

Lincoln's Laws

While in office, Lincoln did much more than lead the Civil War and free slaves. He passed several laws that still affect Americans today:

- The Morrill Act gave public lands to states to be used for higher education purposes.

- The Homestead Act granted 160 acres of public land to anyone who settled on it for five years.

- The Pacific Railroad Act led to the first transcontinental railroad.

- The Internal Revenue Act slowed inflation by introducing federal income tax.

- The Legal Tender Act created the first national paper currency.

Lincoln listened to the advice of his Cabinet. He kept the proclamation a secret, waiting for a moment when the Union had the upper hand in the war. He began decreasing McClellan's control of the Union's armies, trying to find a better general. He tried several other people but could not find anyone to do the job right. Finally, McClellan's army had a stroke of good fortune on September 17, 1862. They trapped Robert E. Lee's Confederate army at the Battle of Antietam in Maryland, forcing it to retreat back to Virginia. Lincoln recognized the battle as the victory he was waiting for.

His chance had come.

On September 22, 1862, Lincoln announced his plan to issue a proclamation of emancipation for all slaves in the Confederate States. The announcement changed the nature of the war.

Abraham Lincoln

BY THE PRESIDENT OF THE UNITED STATES OF AMERICA.

A Proclamation.

Whereas, on the twenty-second day of September, in the year of our Lord one thousand eight hundred and sixty-two, a proclamation was issued by the President of the United States, containing, among other things, the following, to wit:

"That on the first day of January, in the year of our Lord one thousand eight hundred and sixty-three, all persons held as slaves within any State or designated part of a State, the people whereof shall then be in rebellion against the United States, shall be then, thenceforward, and forever, free; and the Executive government of the United States, including the military and naval authority thereof, will recognize and maintain the freedom of such persons, and will do no act or acts to repress such persons, or any of them, in any efforts they may make for their actual freedom.

"That the Executive will, on the first day of January aforesaid, by proclamation, designate the States and parts of States, if any, in which the people thereof, respectively, shall then be in rebellion against the United States; and the fact that any State, or the people thereof, shall on that day be in good faith represented in the Congress of the United States, by members chosen thereto at elections wherein a majority of the qualified voters of such State shall have participated, shall, in the absence of strong countervailing testimony, be deemed conclusive evidence that such State, and the people thereof, are not then in rebellion against the United States."

Now, therefore, I, ABRAHAM LINCOLN, PRESIDENT OF THE UNITED STATES, by virtue of the power in me vested as commander-in-chief of the army and navy of the United States, in time of actual armed rebellion against the authority and government of the United States, and as a fit and necessary war measure for suppressing said rebellion, do, on this first day of January, in the year of our Lord one thousand eight hundred and sixty-three, and in accordance with my purpose so to do, publicly proclaimed for the full period of one hundred days from the day first above mentioned, order and designate as the States and parts of States wherein the people thereof, respectively, are this day in rebellion against the United States, the following, to wit: ARKANSAS, TEXAS, LOUISIANA, (except the Parishes of St. Bernard, Plaquemines, Jefferson, St. John, St. Charles, St. James, Ascension, Assumption, Terre Bonne, Lafourche, St. Mary, St. Martin, and Orleans, including the City of New Orleans,) MISSISSIPPI, ALABAMA, FLORIDA, GEORGIA, SOUTH CAROLINA, NORTH CAROLINA, AND VIRGINIA, (except the forty-eight counties designated as West Virginia, and also the counties of Berkeley, Accomac, Northampton, Elizabeth City, York, Princess Ann, and Norfolk, including the cities of Norfolk and Portsmouth,) and which excepted parts are for the present left precisely as if this proclamation were not issued.

And by virtue of the power and for the purpose aforesaid, I do order and declare that all persons held as slaves within said designated States and parts of States are and henceforward shall be free; and that the Executive government of the United States, including the military and naval authorities thereof, will recognize and maintain the freedom of said persons.

And I hereby enjoin upon the people so declared to be free to abstain from all violence, unless in necessary self-defence; and I recommend to them that, in all cases when allowed, they labor faithfully for reasonable wages.

And I further declare and make known that such persons, of suitable condition, will be received into the armed service of the United States, to garrison forts, positions, stations, and other places, and to man vessels of all sorts in said service.

And upon this act, sincerely believed to be an act of justice warranted by the Constitution upon military necessity, I invoke the considerate judgment of mankind and the gracious favor of Almighty God.

In witness whereof I have hereunto set my hand and caused the seal of the United States to be affixed.

[L. S.] Done at the CITY OF WASHINGTON this first day of January, in the year of our Lord one thousand eight hundred and sixty-three, and of the Independence of the United States of America the eighty-seventh.

Abraham Lincoln

By the President:

William H. Seward, Secretary of State.

Lincoln's Emancipation Proclamation

Chapter 8

Abraham Lincoln giving his Gettysburg Address

Emancipation Proclamation and Gettysburg Address

On January 1, 1863, Abraham Lincoln signed the Emancipation Proclamation. The proclamation declared that "all persons held as

Abraham Lincoln

slaves within any State or designated part of a State … in rebellion against the United States, shall be then, thenceforward, and forever, free."[1]

The language Lincoln used in the Emancipation Proclamation is much plainer than his usual eloquent style. He may have chosen straightforward language so that the meaning of the message would not be overshadowed by fancy wording.

The challenge of the Emancipation Proclamation was that it applied to areas where Lincoln had no authority. Only winning the war would give Lincoln's proclamation power. The Emancipation Proclamation raised the stakes of the Civil War. If restored, the Union would be a different place than it had been before the war. The only way for the South to preserve the institution of slavery would be by winning the war. If the Union did not win, the Emancipation Proclamation would mean nothing in the Confederate States.

Thanksgiving Day

On October 3, 1863, Abraham Lincoln declared a new national holiday. Thanksgiving Day is not celebrated on a specific date, but a particular day: the fourth Thursday of November.

Lincoln remained focused on ending the war. Occasionally, he visited the Union front. He met with McClellan several times and was never very pleased with what he found. Lincoln replaced McClellan with Ambrose Burnside. Burnside was not a good leader either. Burnside lost a battle against Lee even though he had 15,000 troops and Lee had only 5,000. Lincoln then replaced Burnside with Joseph "Fighting Joe" Hooker. An eager general, Hooker turned out to be as unsuccessful as McClellan and Burnside at engaging Lee's army. Hooker quickly resigned. Lincoln tried George Gordon Meade next.

Meade led the Union army to a critical victory.

> **Signing the Proclamation**
>
> On the morning of January 1, 1863, Lincoln signed the Emancipation Proclamation. As he reviewed the document, he noticed a mistake. The document would have to be recopied, but Lincoln had many guests waiting for him to join them for a New Year's celebration. While his staff prepared a new copy of the proclamation, Lincoln went to greet his guests. Later in the day, Lincoln returned to sign the document. He picked up the pen, but his hand shook each time he tried to put it to the paper. Lincoln set the pen down. "I have been shaking hands since nine o'clock this morning, and my right arm is almost paralyzed," he told the few people in the room with him. An unsteady signature, he said, might make it seem that he had hesitated, when in fact "my whole soul is in it." After a moment, Lincoln again picked up the pen and signed his name deliberately. "That will do," he said.[2]
>
> Today, the final, signed copy of the Emancipation Proclamation is in the National Archives in Washington, D.C. The pen Lincoln used was given to Massachusetts Senator Charles Sumner and is now in the Massachusetts Historical Society. The inkwell is now in the Lincoln Museum in Fort Wayne, Indiana.

Abraham Lincoln

On July 1, 1863, a small skirmish at Gettysburg, Pennsylvania, escalated into a three-day battle that was the turning point of the war. At the end of the battle, Meade allowed Lee's army to retreat south, beyond the Potomac River. Meade boasted of "driving the enemy from our soil." Lincoln was upset with Meade for allowing Lee's army to escape, but he was more upset about Meade's attitude. "The whole country is our soil," Lincoln declared in response to Meade's excitement.[3] Lincoln drafted a reprimanding letter to Meade but ultimately decided not to send it. Lincoln did not want to risk offending the best general he had found so far.

Shortly after Meade's victory at Gettysburg, an active young military leader, Ulysses S. Grant, led Union soldiers to capture Vicksburg, Mississippi. Grant's leadership on the western front of the war had made a big difference to the Union's progress. Lincoln took note of Grant. So many of Lincoln's commanding officers were struggling. It was a relief to have one succeed, even if Grant's methods were a bit different. Grant was a scruffy character who did not seek to call attention to himself.

The loss of so many troops at Gettysburg and other recent battles created a need for new recruits, but the

Emancipation Proclamation had splintered Northerners' support for the war. Some thought Lincoln had overstepped his bounds by declaring emancipation. Others believed he had not acted soon enough. Still others were simply tired of the fighting. There were not enough willing volunteers to meet the need for soldiers. The Conscription Act of 1863 broadened the government's ability to draft civilians into military service. In New York City, riots broke out in response to the military draft.

Union soldiers fresh from the battlefield at Gettysburg went to New York to settle the rioters. The soldiers believed in the draft, and they stood behind Lincoln by helping to enforce it. Lincoln had carefully considered how the Emancipation Proclamation would be received within the Union army ranks. He knew that the vast majority of soldiers respected and supported him, regardless of their feelings about slavery. Lincoln believed that emancipation would help the cause more than it would hurt it. He was proven right.

National Draft

Lincoln was the first president to resort to a national draft. The Militia Act of 1862 (July 17) and the Conscription Act of 1863 (March 5) allowed Lincoln to compel citizens to enter the Union army.

Abraham Lincoln

Troops camping out at the White House

    Lincoln understood that keeping the respect and support of his soldiers would help him keep the respect and support of the citizens. Throughout the war, he remained closely involved with even the lowest-ranked soldiers, accepting their letters, responding to their concerns and requests, and even meeting with hundreds of them individually. Lincoln regularly

Essential Lives

visited the troops, who thought him funny looking but sincere. "On horseback in coattails and [a] stovepipe hat he cut a ludicrously elongated figure," one witness wrote.[4] But his awkward manner and plain-spoken attitude convinced the troops of his genuine concern.

Lincoln's efforts paid off. The soldiers stood by him. They wrote letters to their families and friends, defending the moral implications of emancipation. Injured soldiers who returned to their hometowns spoke to their communities to support the cause. The soldiers read newspapers, listened to speeches, and debated the deep moral issues of the war among themselves. Soldiers were some of Lincoln's greatest fans.

In November 1863, Lincoln was invited to make some remarks at the dedication ceremony for a soldiers' cemetery on the Gettysburg battlefield. He knew this speech would be an opportunity to express the heart of the Union mission and to put the turmoil and the great loss of life into perspective. The day before the dedication, Lincoln

Writing the Gettysburg Address

Contrary to popular belief, Lincoln did not really write the Gettysburg Address on the back of an envelope while riding in the carriage on the way to the battlefield. It would have been too bumpy to write legibly. The speech was prepared at the White House several days in advance.

Abraham Lincoln

traveled 80 miles (129 km) from the nation's capital to Gettysburg. The trip was a moment when he had to place his duty to his country ahead of his duty as a husband and father. The Lincolns' young son, Tad, had fallen ill, and Mary Lincoln was terrified of losing him. It must have been difficult for Lincoln to leave his family at that time, especially since two sons had already died from illnesses. Still, he knew how important this speech would be.

Lincoln's speech at Gettysburg on November 19, 1863, remains one of the great speeches of all time. In two brief minutes, he summed up the emotions, beliefs, and goals of the Union's cause. Lincoln began by reminding citizens what the Union was all about. Then he spoke about the war, honoring the courage and sacrifice of the soldiers above all else, saying,

> *Four score and seven years ago, our fathers brought forth on this continent a new nation, conceived in liberty and dedicated to the proposition that "all men are created equal". … The brave men, living and dead, who struggled here, have consecrated [this ground], far above our poor power to add or detract. The world will little note, nor long remember what we say here, but it can never forget what they did here.*[5]

With characteristic modesty, Lincoln tried to downplay his own role in the war and even his ability to honor the soldiers' sacrifice. Lincoln was wrong about one thing: the world has not yet forgotten what he said at Gettysburg.

Abraham Lincoln

Four score and seven years ago our fathers brought forth upon this continent, a new nation, conceived in Liberty, and dedicated to the proposition that all men are created equal.

Now we are engaged in a great civil war, testing whether that nation, or any nation so conceived, and so dedicated, can long endure. We are met on a great battle-field of that war. We have come to dedicate a portion of that field, as a final resting place for those who here gave their lives, that that nation might live. It is altogether fitting and proper that we should do this.

But, in a larger sense, we can not dedicate — we can not consecrate — we can not hallow — this ground. The brave men, living and dead, who struggled here, have consecrated it, far above our poor power to add or detract. The world will little note, nor long remember, what we say here, but it can never forget what they did here. It is for us, the living, rather, to be dedicated here to the unfinished work which they who fought here, have, thus far, so nobly advanced. It is rather for us to be here dedicated to the great task remaining before us — that from these honored dead we take increased devotion to that cause for which they here gave the last full measure of devotion — that we here highly resolve that these dead shall not have died in vain — that this nation, under God, shall have a new birth of freedom — and that, government of the people, by the people, for the people, shall not perish from the earth.

Lincoln's Gettysburg Address in his own handwriting

Chapter 9

Lincoln gives his second inaugural address

A Second Term

The high human cost of the war took a great toll on Lincoln. The loss of soldiers was more to him than mere numbers and battle plans. He felt the grief that plagued families across the nation. Lincoln and his wife often visited the hospitals where

Abraham Lincoln

wounded soldiers rested. The visits were important to Lincoln and encouraging to the soldiers, but they made him long for a way to end the war.

By the beginning of 1864, the war had gone on for nearly three years, and there was a great deal of fighting still ahead. It was time for Lincoln to think about reelection. The thought of losing his office disturbed Lincoln deeply. If he lost the election, it would likely spell the defeat of the Union. It would mean that Northerners were unhappy with the direction of the war, and whoever they elected would likely take the war in a different direction. A new administration might lift Lincoln's proclamation of emancipation or end the war without retaking the South for the Union. Lincoln's fears were well-founded. The unrest within the North and the divisions created by his emancipation order threatened an electoral upset.

Lincoln vowed to his Cabinet members that, if he lost the election, he would work with the new president-elect to end the war before he left office. He wrote to his

White House Stables Fire

On February 10, 1864, the White House stables caught fire and burned to the ground. Lincoln ran into the blaze to save his sons' horses. He "jumped over the boxwood hedge, threw open the stable door, and tried to get the horses out."[1] But the fire was too far gone. He was not able to free the four horses and two ponies inside. As the fire died down, Lincoln stood in the Green Room of the White House and wept over the loss of the animals.

advisors in a memorandum:

> *It seems exceedingly probable that this Administration will not be re-elected. Then it will be my duty to so co-operate with the President-elect as to save the Union between the election and the inauguration; as he will have secured his election on such ground that he can not possibly save it afterwards.*[2]

At that point, Lincoln really believed he would not be reelected. He thought his Democratic successor would call for an immediate end to the war. Such a platform would result in two separate nations—the United States of America and the Confederate States of America. The platfom would also actively bring back slavery. Three years of war and thousands of lives lost would come to mean nothing, and the country would return to the way things had been on Lincoln's inauguration day.

As it turned out, Lincoln was wrong about the Democrats' plans. During the 1864 campaign, they ran

Famous Firsts

On the day of Lincoln's second inaugural ceremony, March 4, 1865, a parade moved from the White House to the Capitol building to meet Lincoln, who was already in the Senate wing of the building. It was a gray and blustery day. Firemen from Philadelphia and Washington, D.C., marched in the parade. A group of labor union members rode in a wagon, scattering programs detailing the day's events. In that parade, for the first time in the nation's capital, a battalion of African-American troops from the Union army marched as inaugural guards.

Abraham Lincoln

on a platform of peace. They promised to restore the Union, but not by continuing the war. In order to bring the two halves of the country back together, they planned to negotiate and compromise with the Confederacy over the issue of slavery. The Democrats decided to run McClellan as their presidential candidate. Lincoln knew from his experience working with McClellan as a general that McClellan's presidential leadership would likely be a disaster.

Lincoln's Reelection
Before Lincoln's election victory in 1864, no president had won reelection since Andrew Jackson in 1832.

As the campaign went on, the war began going better for the Union. In March 1864, Lincoln finally found the general-in-chief that he needed: Ulysses S. Grant. Grant had caught Lincoln's attention earlier in the war with his repeated successes leading troops in the western part of the country. Under Grant's excellent strategic leadership, Union armies began to gain ground in ways they had never been able to manage before. For the first time in the course of the war, the Union was on top.

The Union's progress came at a great cost. Tens of thousands of soldiers died in battle as Grant marched the Union army into the South. The high number of casualties rattled Northerners' commitment to the war. Lincoln's fears of an election defeat increased.

On September 2, 1864, General William Sherman led Union troops into Atlanta, Georgia, capturing the city after a long, slow effort. Days later, Major General Philip Sheridan's troops took control of the Shenandoah Valley of Virginia after crucial battles at Winchester, Fisher's Hill, and Cedar Creek. These military victories renewed hope throughout the North.

The presidential election took place November 4, 1864. Lincoln won all but three of the Northern states, which was enough to ensure him a landslide victory.

Lincoln's Second Inaugural Address

After being elected to a second term as president of the United States in November 1864, Lincoln gave his second inaugural address March 4, 1865. The state of the nation was worse than when Lincoln gave his first inaugural address. When first elected president, Lincoln worried about the possibility of war and keeping the Union together. Four years later, Lincoln was fighting to lead the North to victory over the South in the Civil War, end slavery, and reunite the divided nation.

In his speech, Lincoln spoke with the struggles of the last few years in mind:

With malice toward none; with charity for all; with firmness in the right, as God gives us to see the right, let us strive on to finish the work we are in; to bind up the nation's wounds; to care for him who shall have borne the battle, and for his widow, and his orphan—to do all which may achieve and cherish a just and a lasting peace, among ourselves, and with all nations.[3]

Abraham Lincoln

Lincoln's strongest support came from the Union army. The vast majority of soldiers voted for him.

Knowing he now had four more years as president, Lincoln began looking ahead to reconstruction. His reelection ensured that the war would continue. All signs pointed to a Union victory, though it was far from a certainty. Lincoln's Proclamation of Amnesty and Reconstruction promised a presidential pardon to Confederates as long as they took an oath of loyalty to the Union and agreed to abide by the Emancipation Proclamation. Lincoln agreed to allow states back into the Union once 10 percent of their voting population had accepted the oath.

1864 Election Results

The 1864 presidential election votes:

	Lincoln	McClellan
Popular Vote	2,213,665	1,802,237
Soldiers	116,887	33,748
Electoral College	212	21

On March 4, 1865, Lincoln stood on the steps of the Capitol to deliver his second inaugural address. He reflected on the war and the future of the Union. One month later, Lincoln received word that Richmond, Virginia, the Confederate capital city, had been captured by Union forces. On April 4, 1865, Lincoln visited the Confederate capital, walking right into Confederate President Jefferson Davis's study.

Lincoln remained in Richmond for five days awaiting the Confederate surrender, which he was sure would happen soon. Lincoln wrote to Grant, "Gen. Sheridan says 'If the thing is pressed I think that Lee will surrender.' Let the thing be pressed."[4]

After four long years of war, nearly one million soldiers and citizens from both the North and South had died or were wounded from the effort. On April 9, 1865, General Robert E. Lee surrendered to General Ulysses S. Grant in Appomattox, Virginia. The Southern states agreed to once again become part of the United States. The Civil War was over. The Union was saved.

Abraham Lincoln

Confederate General Robert E. Lee surrenders to Union General Ulysses S. Grant at Appomattox, Virginia.

Chapter 10

Abraham Lincoln, April 10, 1865

Assassination and Legacy

On April 14, 1865, just five days after Lee's surrender, President Lincoln and his wife had breakfast at the White House with their oldest son, Robert. Robert had served as an officer under General Grant, and he gave his parents the details

Abraham Lincoln

of the surrender. Later that morning, Lincoln had a meeting with his Cabinet. In the afternoon, Lincoln left the White House to go for a carriage ride with his wife. They went to the naval yard, where ships were docked. Lincoln made a surprise visit aboard the *Montauk*, a warship for the Northern army. That afternoon, Lincoln told his wife,

> We must both be more cheerful in the future; between the war and the loss of our darling Willie, we have both been very miserable.[1]

That evening, Abraham and Mary Lincoln went to Ford's Theatre, where they had reserved seats to see the play *Our American Cousin*, a comedy about an American who inherits a fortune from an English relative. Because of death threats, they had been warned about the safety of going to the theater and other public places. However, the Lincolns knew that people were counting on them to be there. Lincoln had long ago decided that threats would not keep him from living his life and serving his country.

Lincoln's Tomb

Abraham Lincoln is buried in Springfield, Illinois, near his wife, Mary, and three of their four sons: Edward, William, and Thomas (Tad). Lincoln's first son, Robert, is buried in Arlington National Cemetery.

Lincoln's Possessions

In 1937, Lincoln's granddaughter presented a box wrapped in brown paper and tied with string to the Library of Congress. The box was locked in a safe until 1976, when it was finally opened. It contained all of the things that were in Lincoln's pockets at the time of his death.

When he died, Lincoln had these things in his pockets:

- two pairs of glasses in a silver case
- a small piece of velvet cloth, for cleaning eyeglasses
- a large handkerchief with *A. Lincoln* sewn on it
- a pocketknife
- a brown leather wallet containing a Confederate $5 bill and nine newspaper clippings

The Lincolns arrived late for the play. It had already started by the time they reached Ford's Theatre around 8:30 p.m. The small balcony where they sat was decorated with American flag bunting, and there was a rocking chair for Lincoln. The couple slipped into their seats, but as soon as the audience realized the Lincolns had arrived, the action on stage stopped. The band played "Hail to the Chief." Then the performance resumed.

The door to the box where the Lincolns sat was closed during the show, but it was not locked or guarded. For some reason, one of the two men in charge of keeping watch at the door left his post. The other man, named Forbes, let John Wilkes Booth, a popular actor of the day, into the presidential box around 10:15 p.m. Usually, there would have been no reason why a well-known actor should not be let in to see Lincoln. Forbes had no way of

Abraham Lincoln

John Wilkes Booth shoots Abraham Lincoln in a balcony of Ford's Theatre.

knowing that Booth was a pro-slavery Confederate loyalist who had devised an elaborate plot to kill the president.

Booth went in and locked the door behind him. The third act of the play was showing on stage. The audience was laughing, and Lincoln and his wife were holding hands.

John Wilkes Booth stood just a few feet behind the president and pointed a small single-shot pistol at the back of Lincoln's head. Booth pulled the trigger. Lincoln's head fell forward onto his chest. Mary Lincoln screamed.

There was another couple in the balcony sitting with the Lincolns. Henry R. Rathbone was a young army officer. He and his fiancée, Clara Harris, had been invited to go to the play with the Lincolns. When the president was shot, Rathbone jumped up to fend off the attacker. Booth stabbed Rathbone in the arm with a hunting knife then leapt from the balcony onto the stage. He caught the spur of his boot on the bunting when he jumped. He injured his leg, possibly breaking his ankle. When he landed on the stage, Booth yelled, "Sic semper tyrannis!" This Latin phrase was the state motto of Virginia, Booth's home state. It means "Thus always to tyrants."[2]

Booth escaped out the back door of the theater and into the night. A stagehand waited in the alley behind the theater, holding the reins of Booth's horse. He thought he was simply being helpful. He did not know the horse would help the president's assassin get away.

Abraham Lincoln

Inside the theater, people screamed and ran toward the exits. An army surgeon in the audience, Charles A. Leale, tried to help Lincoln, who was still alive. Mary held her husband up in his chair. The doctor and others helped lay the unconscious president on the floor, so they could see how badly he was hurt. He was alive, but barely.

Some people wanted to rush Lincoln back to the White House so that he could be treated by his personal doctor. Dr. Leale and others present knew Lincoln would not survive the rough trip. Instead, he was carried to a small room on the first floor of a boarding house across the street from the theater. William Peterson, the owner of the house, offered one of his bedrooms as a makeshift hospital room.

Ford's Theatre

Today, Ford's Theatre is a part of the National Mall and Memorial Parks, a division of the National Park Service. Visitors can tour the theater and visit the historic Lincoln sites. They can also attend any of the live shows still presented at the theater each year.

Lincoln was so tall that he had to be placed diagonally on the bed. Mrs. Lincoln spent the night in a parlor in another part of the boarding house. Whenever she went in to see her husband, she became so upset that she had to be taken from the room. Robert Lincoln came to the boarding house to be with his parents, but younger brother Tad stayed at the White House.

As news of the shooting spread, people began coming to the boarding house. Many stood outside and prayed, waiting for news. Many of Lincoln's friends and advisors came to pay their respects and to say goodbye. Lincoln had nearly 100 visitors in his final hours.

At 7:22 the next morning, April 15, Abraham Lincoln died. He was 56 years old. In the small room, a Presbyterian minister said a prayer. Robert Lincoln and others

The Lincoln Memorial

The Lincoln Memorial was designed by Henry Bacon in the early 1900s as part of a plan to revitalize Washington, D.C. Groundbreaking ceremonies were held February 12, 1914, the one hundred and fifth anniversary of Lincoln's birthday. The monument is 190 feet (58 m) long, 119 feet (36 m) wide, and 44 feet (13 m) tall (about the height of a four-story building) and carved out of white Colorado yule marble. Its 36 Doric columns represent the number of states in the Union when Lincoln was president.

Sculptor Daniel Chester French began work on the statue of Lincoln in 1914. The statue was intended to be 10 feet (3 m) tall and cast in bronze, but once he saw the size of the monument, French realized the statue needed to be much bigger. He also chose to use marble instead to match the building. The statue is 19 feet (6 m) high and rests on a pedestal 11 feet (3 m) tall. The imposing size is meant to convey strength and confidence.

The monument was completed and dedicated on May 30, 1922. It cost $3 million to create. New York art critic Royal Cortissoz wrote its inscription: "In this temple, as in the hearts of the people for whom he saved the Union, the memory of Abraham Lincoln is enshrined forever."[3]

Abraham Lincoln

who were there wept. Lincoln's secretary of war, Edwin M. Stanton, stood at the foot of the president's bed. Stanton slowly put his hat on and then just as slowly took the hat off. Looking at Lincoln's lifeless body, Stanton simply said, "Now he belongs to the ages."[4]

Word of Lincoln's death spread immediately. The nation mourned the tragic loss of the leader who had brought them through the most trying struggle in the country's history. Thousands flocked to the capital to pay their respects to Abraham Lincoln. His funeral was held in the East Room of the White House on April 19. Lincoln's family then took him back to Springfield, Illinois, for burial. The train carrying Lincoln's body took a route through the North similar to the one that had brought Lincoln to Washington, D.C., in 1861. At every station along the journey, people crowded around to honor their fallen hero. On May 4, 1865, Lincoln

Booth's Conspiracy

John Wilkes Booth was in the audience on April 11, 1865, when Lincoln made a speech in which he said he believed African Americans should have the right to vote. Booth is said to have remarked, "This is the last speech he will ever make."[5]

Booth was a staunch supporter of the Confederate cause and had been plotting against Lincoln for months. His original plan was to kidnap Lincoln and trade him back to the Union in exchange for the release of captured Confederate soldiers. When the war ended before he could make a move, Booth decided instead to kill Lincoln.

was buried in Illinois soil, in the land where he had lived most of his life.

When he said, "Now he belongs to the ages," Stanton could not possibly have known then just how accurate and meaningful his quiet words at Lincoln's deathbed would be. Abraham Lincoln's legacy would live on for the ages. More than 100 years after his death, Lincoln is still one of the most-known, most-studied, and best-loved presidents in American history.

Abraham Lincoln

Lincoln's funeral

Essential Lives

Timeline

1809

Lincoln is born February 12 near Hodgenville, Kentucky.

1816

The Lincoln family moves to Spencer County, Indiana, in December.

1830

The Lincoln family moves to Macon County, Illinois, in March.

1842

Lincoln marries Mary Todd November 4.

1846

Lincoln wins election to the U.S. House of Representatives August 3.

1854

The Kansas-Nebraska Act becomes a law May 30.

Abraham Lincoln

1833

Lincoln becomes postmaster of New Salem, Illinois, May 7.

1834

Lincoln wins election to the Illinois House of Representatives August 4.

1837

Lincoln earns his law license from the Illinois Supreme Court March 1.

1858

Lincoln and Douglas debate throughout the fall while campaigning for a U.S. Senate seat.

1860

Lincoln is elected president November 6.

1861

Lincoln takes the oath of office March 4.

Timeline

1861
Confederate forces fire on Fort Sumter April 12, starting the Civil War.

1862
On September 22, Lincoln announces his plan to free slaves.

1863
Lincoln signs the Emancipation Proclamation January 1.

1865
Congress passes the Thirteenth Amendment, abolishing slavery, January 31.

1865
Lincoln delivers his second inaugural address March 4.

1865
General Lee surrenders April 9; the Civil War ends.

Abraham Lincoln

1863

Union troops win the Battle of Gettysburg, July 1–3.

1863

Lincoln delivers the Gettysburg Address November 19.

1864

Lincoln wins a second term as president November 8.

1865

Lincoln delivers his last public address April 11, in which he suggests that African Americans who fought as Union soldiers should be granted the right to vote.

1865

John Wilkes Booth shoots Lincoln in Ford's Theatre April 14.

1865

Lincoln dies early in the morning of April 15.

Essential Lives

Essential Facts

Date of Birth
February 12, 1809

Place of Birth
Sinking Spring Farm, near Hodgenville, Kentucky

Date of Death
April 15, 1865

Place of Death
Washington, D.C.

Parents
Thomas and Nancy Lincoln

Education
Lincoln had formal schooling equivalent to about a sixth-grade level. He was mostly self-educated.

Marriage
Mary Todd, November 4, 1842

Children
Robert Todd, born 1843
Edward Baker, born 1846
William Wallace, born 1850
Thomas (Tad), born 1853

Career Highlights
- Served in Illinois militia in 1832.
- Elected to Illinois House of Representatives in 1834.
- Elected to a second term in Illinois House of Representatives in 1836.
- Earned law license in 1836.
- Elected to a third term in Illinois House of Representatives in 1838.

Abraham Lincoln

- Elected to a fourth term in Illinois House of Representatives in 1840.
- Elected to U.S. House of Representatives in 1846.
- Elected to Illinois House of Representatives in 1856.
- Elected president of the United States in 1860.
- Elected to a second term as president in 1864.

Societal Contributions
As a state politician, Lincoln worked to improve conditions in Illinois. As president, he worked to improve the entire nation and the lives of its inhabitants, especially the lives of slaves.

Residences
Born in Kentucky, Lincoln moved with his family to Indiana as a toddler, and then to Illinois as a boy. As an adult, Lincoln lived in Illinois until moving to Washington, D.C., to serve as president.

Travels
As a young man, Lincoln traveled down the Mississippi River on a boat twice to deliver goods. As president, Lincoln traveled considerably, particularly during the Civil War.

Conflicts
Lincoln fought for the freedom of slaves; his views on slavery led to the Civil War.

Quote
Lincoln's Gettysburg Address is perhaps his best-known speech. It begins with this famous line: "Four score and seven years ago our fathers brought forth on this continent a new nation, conceived in Liberty and dedicated to the proposition that all men are created equal."

Additional Resources

Select Bibliography

Carwardine, Richard. *Lincoln: A Life of Purpose and Power.* New York: Alfred Knopf, 2006.

Lincoln, Abraham. *The Collected Works of Abraham Lincoln.* Ann Arbor, MI: University of Michigan Digital Library Production Services, 2001.

The Lincoln Log: A Daily Chronology of the Life of Abraham Lincoln. Papers of Abraham Lincoln, Illinois Historic Preservation Agency. 25 Feb. 2007 <http://www.stg.brown.edu/projects/lincoln/index.php>.

Neely, Mark E., Jr. *The Last Best Hope of Earth: Abraham Lincoln and the Promise of America.* Cambridge, MA: Harvard University Press, 1993.

Prokopowicz, Gerald J. *Abraham Lincoln: America's 16th President.* Fort Washington, PA: Eastern National, 1999.

Further Reading

Alter, Judy. *Abraham Lincoln.* Berkeley Heights, NJ: Enslow Publishers, 2002.

Gienapp, William E. *Abraham Lincoln and Civil War America: A Biography.* New York: Oxford University Press, 2002.

Haugen, Brenda. *Abraham Lincoln: Great American President.* Minneapolis, MN: Compass Point Books, 2006.

Abraham Lincoln

Web Links

To learn more about Abraham Lincoln, visit ABDO Publishing Company on the World Wide Web at **www.abdopublishing.com**. Web sites about Abraham Lincoln are featured on our Book Links page. These links are routinely monitored and updated to provide the most current information available.

Places to Visit

Abraham Lincoln Presidential Library and Museum
112 North Sixth Street, Springfield, IL 62701
800-610-2094
www.alplm.org
The Abraham Lincoln Presidential Library and Museum houses a wealth of material about Abraham Lincoln and the history of Illinois. The library's Lincoln Collection includes thousands of items—letters, photographs, historical artifacts—related to Abraham Lincoln. The museum offers tours for adults and children.

The Lincoln Museum
200 East Berry Street, Fort Wayne, IN 46801
260-455-3864
www.thelincolnmuseum.org
The museum celebrates Abraham Lincoln's life and legacy. Visitors can view special exhibits and a permanent collection containing many Lincoln artifacts and plenty of historical information.

Lincoln Memorial
900 Ohio Drive SW, Washington, DC 20024
202-426-6841
Visitors like to walk up the steps and look at the tall statue of Lincoln, and to see the view from those steps. Sometimes, special events are held in front of the Lincoln Memorial.

Glossary

assassination
The murder of a prominent person, usually for political reasons.

campaign
A coordinated effort to get a candidate elected to public office; also describes a series of military actions during a war.

candidate
An individual who seeks to be elected to public office.

commander in chief
Another name for the president of the United States; the person in that position has full authority and command of the country's armed forces.

confederacy
Generally, this word can describe any group of individuals or states that come together for a particular purpose; in the case of the American Civil War, the Confederacy refers to the 11 Southern states that seceded from the Union to form the Confederate States of America.

Democratic Party
One of the major political parties in the 1800s, it was the dominant political force in the United States, supporting states' rights and territorial expansion.

emancipation
The act of freeing someone or something; the Emancipation Proclamation was a legal act guaranteeing African Americans freedom from slavery in the Southern United States.

enterprise
A company that sells goods.

gaunt
Very thin and angular.

imminent
Likely to happen.

inauguration
An act or ceremony to mark the formal start in office.

Kansas-Nebraska Act
A law passed in 1854 that overturned the Missouri Compromise and introduced popular sovereignty by allowing the northwest U.S. territories to determine whether slavery should be legal in their areas.

Abraham Lincoln

legislature
    An organized group of people that has the authority to make laws for a political unit, such as a state or country.

litigation
    The act of resolving a conflict in a court of law.

Louisiana Purchase
    Land extending from the Mississippi River to the Rocky Mountains between the Gulf of Mexico and Canada that was purchased from France on April 30, 1803, for $15 million.

Missouri Compromise
    Passed in 1820, this act brought Missouri into the Union as a slave state and Maine as a free state; it also outlawed the expansion of slavery into the U.S. territories of the northwest, the land where Nebraska and the Dakotas would eventually be.

platform
    The set of ideas, beliefs, goals, and interests that a political candidate uses as the basis of his or her campaign.

popular sovereignty
    Senator Stephen A. Douglas's principle of allowing citizens of U.S. territories to decide whether slavery should be allowed.

proclamation
    An official public announcement.

Republican Party
    A political party formed in the 1850s based on an anti-slavery platform.

secede
    To withdraw or separate from an organization.

slavery
    A condition of being made to submit to a dominating power; in the pre-Civil War American South, African Americans were considered the property of whites who purchased them and were made to work without wages.

Union
    Another name for the United States; during the Civil War, the North.

Whig
    A major political party in the early 1800s, the Whigs supported states' rights and collective self-government by citizens and were wary of too much power going to any one person, such as the president; the party split in the 1850s over the issue of expanding slavery.

Source Notes

Chapter 1. The Road to Greatness

1. Abraham Lincoln, *The Collected Works of Abraham Lincoln,* vol. 4. Ann Arbor, MI: University of Michigan Digital Library Production Services, 2001. 190.

2. Ibid. 129–130.

3. Ibid. 129–130.

4. Ibid. 193.

Chapter 2. Young Lincoln

1. Gerald J. Prokopowicz, *Abraham Lincoln: America's 16th President.* Fort Washington, MD: Eastern National, 1999. 5.

2. Mark E. Neely Jr. *The Encyclopedia of Abraham Lincoln.* New York: McGraw Hill, 1982. 14.

3. Abraham Lincoln, *The Collected Works of Abraham Lincoln,* vol. 2. Ann Arbor, MI: University of Michigan Digital Library Production Services, 2001. 225.

Chapter 3. Lincoln's Early Political Career

1. Mark E. Neely Jr., *The Last Best Hope of Earth: Abraham Lincoln and the Promise of America.* Cambridge, MA: Harvard University Press, 1993. 7.

2. Richard Carwardine, *Lincoln: A Life of Purpose and Power.* New York: Alfred Knopf, 2006. 9.

3. Gerald J. Prokopowicz, *Abraham Lincoln: America's 16th President.* Fort Washington, MD: Eastern National, 1999. 9.

4. Abraham Lincoln, *The Collected Works of Abraham Lincoln,* vol. 2. Ann Arbor, MI: University of Michigan Digital Library Production Services, 2001. 2.

Chapter 4. Lincoln as Husband and Father

1. *The Lincoln Log: A Daily Chronology of the Life of Abraham Lincoln.* Papers of Abraham Lincoln, Illinois Historic Preservation Agency. 25 Feb. 2007 <http://www.stg.brown.edu/projects/lincoln/index.php>.

2. Gerald J. Prokopowicz, *Abraham Lincoln: America's 16th President.* Fort Washington, MD: Eastern National, 1999. 31.

3. Abraham Lincoln, *The Collected Works of Abraham Lincoln,* vol. 1. Ann Arbor, MI: University of Michigan Digital Library Production Services, 2001. 382.

Chapter 5. Lincoln Returns to Politics

1. Abraham Lincoln, *The Collected Works of Abraham Lincoln,* vol. 2. Ann Arbor, MI: University of Michigan Digital Library Production Services, 2001. 222.

2. Gerald J. Prokopowicz, *Abraham Lincoln: America's 16th President.* Fort Washington, MD: Eastern National, 1999. 19.

3. Richard Carwardine, *Lincoln: A Life of Purpose and Power.* New York: Alfred Knopf, 2006. 76–77.

4. Gerald J. Prokopowicz, *Abraham Lincoln: America's 16th President.* Fort Washington, MD: Eastern National, 1999. 16.

5. Ibid. 20.

6. Abraham Lincoln, *The Collected Works of Abraham Lincoln,* vol. 2. Ann Arbor, MI: University of Michigan Digital Library Production Services, 2001. 255.

Chapter 6. To the Presidency

1. Gerald J. Prokopowicz, *Abraham Lincoln: America's 16th President.* Fort Washington, MD: Eastern National, 1999. 19.

Source Notes Continued

2. Mark E. Neely Jr. *The Abraham Lincoln Encyclopedia.* New York: McGraw-Hill, 1982. 72.

3. "Article II, Section 1," *Constitution of the United States of America,* National Constitution Center, 7 June 2007 <http://www.constitutioncenter.org/constitution/details_explanation.php?link=079&const=02_art_02&keyword=oath+of+office>.

4. Gerald J. Prokopowicz, *Abraham Lincoln: America's 16th President.* Fort Washington, MD: Eastern National, 1999. 7.

Chapter 7. A Nation Divided

1. Gerald J. Prokopowicz, *Abraham Lincoln: America's 16th President.* Fort Washington, MD: Eastern National, 1999. 29.

2. Abraham Lincoln, *The Collected Works of Abraham Lincoln,* vol. 5. New Brunswick, NJ: Rutgers University Press, 1953. 389.

Chapter 8. Emancipation Proclamation and Gettysburg Address

1. Richard Carwardine, *Lincoln: A Life of Purpose and Power.* New York: Alfred Knopf, 2006. 219.

2. Gerald J. Prokopowicz, "The Emancipation Inkwell," *Lincoln Lore* Winter 1996, The Lincoln Museum, 25 Feb. 2007 <http://www.thelincolnmuseum.org/new/publications/1843.html>.

3. Gerald J. Prokopowicz, *Abraham Lincoln: America's 16th President.* Fort Washington, MD: Eastern National, 1999. 40.

4. Richard Carwardine, *Lincoln: A Life of Purpose and Power.* New York: Alfred Knopf, 2006. 285.

5. Abraham Lincoln, *The Collected Works of Abraham Lincoln,* vol. 2. Ann Arbor, MI: University of Michigan Digital Library Production Services, 2001. n.p.

Abraham Lincoln

Chapter 9. A Second Term

1. *The Lincoln Log: A Daily Chronology of the Life of Abraham Lincoln.* Papers of Abraham Lincoln, Illinois Historic Preservation Agency. 25 Feb. 2007 <http://www.stg.brown.edu/projects/lincoln/index.php>.

2. Mark E. Neely Jr., *The Abraham Lincoln Encyclopedia.* New York: McGraw-Hill, 1982. 172.

3. Gerald J. Prokopowicz, *Abraham Lincoln: America's 16th President.* Fort Washington, MD: Eastern National, 1999. 49.

4. Abraham Lincoln, *The Collected Works of Abraham Lincoln,* vol. 8. Ann Arbor, MI: University of Michigan Digital Library Production Services, 2001. 392.

Chapter 10. Assassination and Legacy

1. Tanya Lee Stone, *Abraham Lincoln: A Photographic Story of a Life.* New York: Dorling Kindersley, 2005. 113.

2. Doris Kearns Goodwin, *Team of Rivals: The Political Genius of Abraham Lincoln.* New York: Simon & Schuster, 2005. 789.

3. Mark E. Neely Jr., *The Abraham Lincoln Encyclopedia.* New York: McGraw-Hill, 1982. 190.

4. *The Lincoln Log: A Daily Chronology of the Life of Abraham Lincoln.* Papers of Abraham Lincoln, Illinois Historic Preservation Agency. 25 Feb. 2007 <http://www.stg.brown.edu/projects/lincoln/index.php>.

5. Tanya Lee Stone, *Abraham Lincoln: A Photographic Story of a Life.* New York, orling Kindersley, 2005. 111.

Index

Anderson, Robert, 59
Antietam, MD, 58, 66
Anti-Nebraska speeches, 40, 42
Appomattox, VA, 84-85
Armstrong, Duff, 33
assassination, 55, 86-94

Battle of Bull Run, 61-62
Bedell, Grace, 10-11
Bell, John, 51-52
Berry, William F., 25-26
Black Hawk War, 18, 23-25
Booth, John Wilkes, 88-90, 93
Border states, 52-53, 60
Breckinridge, John C., 51-52
Burnside, Ambrose, 70

Cartwright, Peter, 34
Chief Black Hawk, 23
Christian, 34
Civil War, 9, 11, 52-53, 58-61, 68-77, 81-85
Confederate flag, 52, 59
Confederate States of America, 9, 52, 56
Cooper Union, 49, 57

Davis, Jefferson, 9, 52, 83
Democratic Party, 40-42, 80-81
Douglas, Stephen A., 38-45, 51-52
Dred Scott decision, 42

election, 25, 45, 52, 79-83
Ellsworth, Elmer, 59
Emancipation Proclamation, 64-72, 83

farewell address, 13
Ford's Theatre, 87-91

Fort Sumter, 59-61

"Gettysburg Address," 68, 74-76
Globe Tavern, 32
Grant, Ulysses S., 71, 81-85
Greeley, Horace, 65

Hodgenville, KY, 15
Honest Abe, 27
Hooker, Joseph "Fighting Joe," 70
"House Divided" speech, 43

Illinois House of Representatives, 22, 25, 27
Illinois militia, 23-24
inaugural address
   first, 55-56
   second, 78, 82-83

Jackson, Thomas "Stonewall," 63, 81

Kansas-Nebraska Act, 38-42
Knob Creek, KY, 15

Lee, Robert E., 63, 66, 70-71, 84
Lexington, KY, 31
Lincoln Log, 7
Lincoln, Abraham
   appearance, 9-11
   birth, 15
   careers, 17-20, 26
   death, 92-94
   education, 17-18
   father, 32-33, 35-36, 75
   husband, 31-32, 75
   marriage, 32
   patent, 23

Abraham Lincoln

penny, 62
tomb, 87
Lincoln, Edward Baker (son), 33
Lincoln, Nancy Hanks (mother), 15-16
Lincoln, Robert Todd (son), 32-33
Lincoln, Sarah Bush Johnston (stepmother), 17, 21
Lincoln, Thomas (father), 15-17
Lincoln, Thomas (Tad), 36, 75
Lincoln, William (Willie), 36, 63, 87
Lincoln-Douglas debates of 1858, 42-46
Louisiana Territory, 39
Lovejoy, Elijah, 27

Macon County, IL, 19
McClellan, George B., 63, 66, 69-70, 81
Meade, George Gordon, 70-71
Mississippi River, 19, 23
Missouri Compromise, 38

New Salem, IL, 19, 25-26

Our American Cousin, 87
Owens, Mary, 31

Pigeon Creek, IN, 16
Proclamation of Amnesty and Reconstruction, 83

Rathbone, Henry R., 90
"Rail Splitter," 51
Republican National Convention, 42, 50
Republican Party, 42, 53

Richmond, VA, 83
Rutledge, Ann, 30

Sangamo Journal, 23-24
Sangamon County, IL, 25
Sinking Spring Farm, 15
slavery, 8, 11, 15-16, 19, 27-28, 39-46, 53-54, 64-65
Springfield, IL, 7, 23, 26-27, 30-32, 35, 54, 93
Stanton, Edwin M., 93-94
Stuart, John Todd, 26, 31

Taylor, Zachary, 35
Todd, Mary (wife). *See* Mary Todd Lincoln, 28-29, 31-37, 51, 60, 63, 75, 87, 90-91

Union, organization of, 11-12, 39, 52-56

Washington, D.C., 7, 12, 35, 54-55, 62-63, 93-92
Whig(s), 28, 33-35, 41-42
White House, 32, 59, 63, 73, 79, 86-87, 91-93
Wide Awakes, 49

Young Men's Lyceum, 27

• 111 •

About the Author

Kekla Magoon has a Master of Fine Arts in Writing for Children and Young Adults from Vermont College. Her work includes many different kinds of writing, but she especially enjoys writing historical fiction and nonfiction. When she is not writing books for children, Kekla works with non-profit organizations and helps with fundraising for youth programs.

Photo Credits

Abraham Lincoln Presidential Library and Museum, cover, 3, 6, 13, 21, 22, 29, 30, 37, 38, 41, 44, 47, 48, 57, 58, 67, 68, 77, 78, 86, 96 (top), 96 (bottom), 97 (top), 97 (bottom), 98 (top), 99 (top); Northwind Picture Archives, 14, 61, 73, 85, 89, 95, 98 (bottom), 99 (bottom).